THE SONG OF SOLOMON

THE CLASSIC BIBLE BOOKS SERIES

The Song of Solomon: Love Poetry of the Spirit
Introduced and Edited by Lawrence Boadt;
Foreword by John Updike

The Hebrew Prophets: Visionaries of the Ancient World
Introduced and Edited by Lawrence Boadt;
Foreword by Desmond Tutu

The Great Sayings of Jesus: Proverbs, Parables and Prayers
Introduced and Edited by John Drane;
Foreword by Richard Holloway

The Gospel of St John: The Story of the Son of God
Introduced and Edited by John Drane;
Foreword by Piers Paul Read

Forthcoming

The Book of Job: Why Do the Innocent Suffer?
Introduced and Edited by Lawrence Boadt;
Foreword by Alice Thomas Ellis

Genesis: The Book of Beginnings
Introduced and Edited by Lawrence Boadt;
Foreword by Sara Maitland

The Psalms: Ancient Poetry of the Spirit
Introduced and Edited by Lawrence Boadt and F. F. Bruce;
Foreword by R. S. Thomas

Sayings of the Wise: The Legacy of King Solomon
Introduced and Edited by Lawrence Boadt;
Foreword by Libby Purves

Stories from the Old Testament: Volume I
Introduced and Edited by Lawrence Boadt;
Foreword by Monica Furlong

Stories from the Old Testament: Volume II
Introduced and Edited by Lawrence Boadt;
Foreword by Morris West

The New Testament Epistles: Early Christian Wisdom
Introduced and Edited by John Drane;
Foreword by Roger McGough

Revelation: The Apocalypse of St John
Introduced and Edited by John Drane;
Foreword by Richard Harries

++

THE SONG OF SOLOMON
Love Poetry of the Spirit

++

INTRODUCED AND EDITED BY LAWRENCE BOADT
FOREWORD BY JOHN UPDIKE

St. Martin's Griffin
New York

ISBN 0-312-22212-2 cloth
ISBN 0-312-22079-0 paperback

Library of Congress Cataloging-in-Publication Data
is available from the Library of Congress.

First published in Great Britain by Lion Publishing plc, 1997.
First St. Martin's Griffin edition: June 1999
10 9 8 7 6 5 4 3 2 1

Contents

ACKNOWLEDGMENTS

The introduction has been reprinted from *Reading the Old Testament* by Lawrence Boadt © 1984 by The Missionary Society of St Paul the Apostle in the State of New York. Used by permission of Paulist Press.

The text of 'The Song of Solomon in Literature' has been selected from *A Dictionary of Biblical Tradition in English Literature*, edited by David Lyle Jeffrey, copyright © 1992 by permission of Wm B. Eerdmans Publishing Co.

The text of The Song of Solomon has been taken from the Authorised Version of the Bible (the King James Bible), the rights of which are vested in the Crown, by permission of Wm B. Eerdmans Publishing Co.

Extract from Annie Dillard has been reproduced from *Holy the Firm*, published by Harper Collins: page 31.

Foreword

Of all the Bible's chapters, none is more surprising and pagan than The Song of Solomon – in Hebrew, *Shir Hashrim*, which the Vulgate translated as *Canticum Canticorum* and some English versions as The Song of Songs. Its dating is difficult. After the Babylonian exile of the sixth century BC, Hebrew was slowly replaced by Aramaic as the language of Palestine; to judge by the proportion of Aramaicized expressions, The Song of Solomon comes fairly late in the process, around the third century BC. Its references to Solomon, who reigned in the tenth century BC, partake of the fabulous and folkloric. His wedding is not elsewhere mentioned in the Bible; the lovers use his golden reign as one of the idyllic settings in which their love is exalted. Yet ancient elements exist in the text. Tirzah, evoked along with Jerusalem, had not been the capital of Israel since the century after Solomon. Certain formulae ('His left hand should be under my head, and his right hand should embrace me') and the emphasis on the spring season and the dialogue form all suggest a derivation from Mesopotamian fertility rites, celebrating a marriage between the king and a goddess, that date back to the third millennium BC. A modern Arabic term, *wasf*, denotes ritual exchanges of songs praising the beloved's beauty, songs that persist at betrothal ceremonies, like western toasts.

The Song, which never once mentions God, was included in the Bible most probably because, like Proverbs and Ecclesiastes and Job, it was a treasure of Hebrew literature. No other love poem from this literature survives. Its attribution to Solomon gave it the protection of a revered historical name. An early commentator, Rabbi Akiva (died AD135), claimed that 'the whole world is not worth the day on which the Song of Songs was given to Israel; for all the writings are holy, but the Song of Songs is the holiest of the holy.' Nevertheless, he read it allegorically, as really about the love between God and Israel. Christian commentators, with more of an anti-sexual bias than the Hebrew scribes, for two millennia sought to explain away the Song's carnal content; the beloved's two breasts became Moses and Aaron in one interpretation, and the Old and New

Testaments in another. A Bible I bought in England in 1955 blandly heads the verses, at the top of the page, 'The church's love of Christ' and 'Christ's love of the church'.

Now, one would hope, Christians can read the Song as a hymn to human love, including a virtual worship of the body of the other. Three voices speak: a young female, called the Shulamite; her lover, from whom she is intermittently separated; and a chorus. The chorus, one theory runs, consists of the women in Solomon's harem, wherein the sun-blackened Shulamite has been enlisted though she longs for her shepherd lover; she searches the city for him and is captured by watchmen who beat her and take away her veil. But it is impossible to make such a cogent dramatic situation fit every verse; the lovers' voices change tense and context in a manner that seems – not inappropriately – delirious. The Song of Solomon has traditionally been printed without differentiating the speakers, compounding a confusion that no translation can eliminate. The original Hebrew is, according to the introduction by Ariel and Chana Bloch to their 1995 translation, exceptionally compressed, elliptical, and rich in rare words and *hapax legomena* – words that occur nowhere else and whose meaning must be conjectured. It is also the most vernacular Hebrew in the Bible, and contains a number of words of Persian and Greek origin, as well as similarities with the pastoral idylls of Theocritus, a Greek poet who wrote in Alexandria in the first half of the third century BC.

Instead of a modern version like that of the Blochs, we have chosen to use, without the traditional verse numbering and with speakers identified, the King James Version. Phrases of its ringing archaic English still permeate the language: 'I am black, but comely'; 'Stay me with flagons, comfort me with apples'; 'The voice of the turtle is heard in our land'; 'Take us the foxes, the little foxes, that spoil the vines: for our vines have tender grapes'. The Song's erotic magnificence crests in well-known verses near the end:

> Thy navel is like a round goblet,
> which wanteth not liquor:
> thy belly is like an heap of wheat
> set about with lilies.

> Thy two breasts are like two young roes
> that are twins.

In the next verses, however, the Jacobean rendition of Hebraic concreteness strikes the modern ear as absurd:

> Thy neck is as a tower of ivory;
> thine eyes like the fishpools in Heshbon,
> by the gate of Bathrabbim:
> thy nose is as the tower of Lebanon
> which looketh toward Damascus.

In another verse, a shift in the language has betrayed the poetry: 'My beloved put in his hand by the hole of the door, and my bowels were moved for him.' But love includes earthiness as well as exaltation, and its spiritual fever embraces the extravagant and does not shun the grotesque.

'I have eaten my honeycomb with my honey,' the lover avows. He exclaims, 'How beautiful are thy feet with shoes,' and likens the joints of her thighs to jewels. He finds the beloved as 'fair as the moon, clear as the sun, and terrible as an army with banners'. And she, even more rapturous, wants him to lie all night between her breasts; her hands upon the handle of the lock she opens to him are wet with myrrh. She conceives him in terms of hard, towering substances: 'His legs are as pillars of marble, set upon sockets of fine gold,' and his countenance 'is as excellent as the cedars' of Lebanon. And she to him is 'a garden inclosed... a spring shut up, a fountain sealed'. The ecstasy of reciprocated desire needs not wait for Freudian interpretation; these voices are dizzily drenched in perfumes, fruits, spices – all of the nature around them brings metaphors to the feasts of their senses. The speed of their heartbeats lives in the rapidity of their crowding similes; the mutual outpouring ends with the Shulamite's cry:

> Make haste, my beloved,
> and be thou like to a roe or to a young hart
> upon the mountains of spices.

This anticipates the last utterance of the New Testament, in Revelation: 'Surely I come quickly. Amen. Even so, come, Lord Jesus.' The yearning for love fills the cosmos.

The Bible would be the poorer if it lacked The Song of Solomon. Its burst of sensual rapture and erotic passion helps ground Biblical humanism on the human creature that exists, under the great frowning imperatives of heaven. Carnal passion has its natural place in the annals of Israel; Judaism recognized that the body is the person, a recognition extended in the strenuous Christian doctrine of the bodily resurrection. A world-picture must include everything that is the case, and the love frenzy of the young – the Shulamite is so young she is accused of having no breasts – completes, along with the cynicism of Ecclesiastes, the despair of Lamentation, the problematics of Job, and the plagues and war-fury of Numbers, the picture. We might even say that, in this era of irrepressible sexual awareness, we trust the Bible a bit more because it contains, in all its shameless, helpless force, The Song of Solomon.

John Updike

INTRODUCTION

The Song of Solomon is one of three books in the Old Testament attributed to Solomon, in this case mainly because his name is mentioned in chapters 3 and 8. In both instances he seems more of a model to follow than an author, and we can safely say that the famous king did not write these songs. Like so many other wisdom books, The Song of Solomon shows signs of being worked and reworked through many centuries. At the oldest level are love poems, perhaps wedding songs, many of which could go back to the time of Solomon. At the latest level are Persian and Greek phrases that indicate additions made after the exile. There seem to be hints of a dialogue between a young lover and his beloved (bride?), and perhaps even a chorus of the daughters of Jerusalem. At least the tradition of identifying different speakers goes back to the Greek translations before the time of Christ. But there is not enough unity among the different songs to say more than that it is a collection extolling the undying power of love between two people.

Researchers studied Arab village life in the late 19th century to find parallels to the ways of ancient Israel that might still be carried on almost unchanged through the intervening centuries. One remarkable parallel to the Song of Solomon was the custom of singing a *wasf*, which was a wedding song about the beauty of a bride's or groom's body. The wedding customs also included a dance with a sword by the bride on the day before her wedding in which she described her own beauty (Song of Solomon 1:5; 2:1). For the week after the wedding, the couple is treated as a king and queen with much feasting and still more songs extolling the bride's beauty (Song of Solomon 4:1–15; 5:10–16). Compare the following Syrian wedding song with Song of Solomon 7:1–4:

Syrian Wedding Song

> Her teeth are like pearls,
> Her neck like the neck of an antelope,
> Her shoulders are firm,

> Her navel like a box of perfumes
>> with all spices flowing from it;
> Her body like strains of silk,
> Her limbs like firm pillars.

Song of Solomon 7:1–4

> Your thighs rounded like a jewel
>> are the work of a master hand.
> Your navel is a rounded bowl
>> that is always filled with wine.
> Your belly is a stack of wheat
>> surrounded by lilies.
> Your breasts are like two fawns,
>> the twins of a gazelle.
> Your neck is like an ivory tower.
> Your eyes like pools in Heshbon.

Such village customs last over many centuries and can help us discover the original setting and use of the Song of Solomon. The religious use of such love songs may even go back to hymns and ceremonies surrounding the sacred marriage rituals of the Canaanite followers of Baal. Certainly, Israel was not the only ancient nation to sing the beauties of the female body (and sometimes of the male). We have examples from both Babylon and Egypt,[1] and Psalm 45 is also a wedding psalm.

But the lusty nature of the songs were scandalous to many of the Jewish rabbis, and as late as the 2nd century AD they still had not fully agreed that the book should be in the sacred canon. One of the deciding factors was the belief that it described allegorically the love of Yahweh for Israel as a beloved bride. The Christian church accepted it quickly for the same reasons – it could easily describe in allegory the love of Christ for the church, or for the soul of the believer. St Bernard of Clairvaux in the 12th century wrote a great number of sermons on the Song of Solomon describing the love of Christ for the soul and the mystical union that came from this love. They have become the classic source for mystical spirituality. Other Christian writers of the Middle Ages saw an allegory of Christ's love for his Blessed Mother. In all of these cases, the later interpretations have gone far beyond the original Old Testament book with its rather graphic description of sexual love as a joyful and positive ideal. But they also underline the power of the book to lead people in all ages to discover that love, sexuality, and creation are gifts of God's goodness.

Lawrence Boadt

Note

1. Ancient Near Eastern Texts 467–69.

THE SONG OF SOLOMON
IN LITERATURE

Images and Quotations

Images and Quotations

Bride, Bridegroom

The one-flesh nuptial union of man and woman and the command to be fruitful and multiply, presented as the primordial divine injunction in Genesis 1:28, are reflected throughout the Old Testament, which is as much a story of marriages and begettings as of any other human activity. Weddings were a principal festal occasion in the Hebrew, as in other Near Eastern cultures, notably the 'wedding-week' celebrations in which the bride and groom were fêted as symbolic 'king' and 'queen' with the singing of lyric songs of praise. A mishnaic passage describes ritual folk dances of courtship performed by 'the daughters of Jerusalem' in connection with the annual festivals of summer harvest and autumnal vintage, and associates the joy of this 'day of espousals' with Israel's joy in the giving of the Law and the building of the Temple. The 'voice of the bridegroom and the bride' in fact became paradigmatic of joy in the land (Jeremiah 33:11), as, conversely, its absence was emblematic of desolation (Jeremiah 7:34; 16:9; 25:10; cf. Revelation 18:3). The rising of the sun in the east was compared to a bridegroom emerging joyfully from the bridechamber (Psalm 19:4–5). This tradition is reflected in nuptial poetry from the Song of Solomon through the epithalamia of the Renaissance, and in descriptive re-creations of traditional Jewish weddings as in the stories of Sholem Aleichem or Chaim Potok's *The Chosen*.

Figurative uses of nuptial imagery from the Bible are many and varied. The image of Israel as bride in her covenant relationship to God, and the period of her Exodus deliverance and the giving of the Law as the time of her espousals, undoubtedly goes back to the period of conflict with Baal worship and the widespread mythos in surrounding cultures of sacred marriage of god and goddess, and the institution of sacred prostitution (see S.N. Kramer, *The Sacred Marriage Rite*, 1969). Hebrew theology substituted for such symbolism the image of Israel herself as corporate bride. Most frequently, the image is encountered in a negative context: Israel has proven to be a faithless bride and has gone 'whoring' after alien gods (e.g., Exodus 34:12;

Leviticus 17:17; 20:7; Deuteronomy 31:16; 1 Chronicles 5:25; Jeremiah 2:32; Ezekiel 16:15); but God is not only a 'jealous' God, he is also a superabundantly loving husband, who will be true to his covenant despite the bride's unfaithfulness, take her back (Hosea 1–2), and establish with her a renewed nuptial bond (Isaiah 54:5; 62:5).

In light of this symbolism, Psalm 45, a royal epithalamium, was interpreted by the rabbis as an allegory of God's betrothal to Israel, exactly as was the Song of Solomon. This allegorization runs through the entire history of Jewish exegesis, from the Targum on Song of Solomon, through the Mishnah and Talmud, the Midrash Rabbah, and all the great Jewish commentators of the Middle Ages and Renaissance; it lies at the heart of the Zohar and other classics of the Cabala, such as Leon Hebraeus' *Dialogues of Love*. In the popular devotional literature of Judaism, the symbolism is most familiar in the image of the Sabbath as Bride of God, as in the Sabbath hymns of Judah Halevi and other religious poets (see *Daily Prayer Book / Ha-Siddur Ha-Shalem,* ed. P. Birnbaum, 1949).

In the gospels the metaphor reappears with a new emphasis on the Messiah as bridegroom. John the Baptist describes himself in relation to the mission of Jesus as 'friend of the bridegroom' (John 3:29). In the synoptics, Jesus himself, answering questions about why his own disciples do not fast, says, 'Can the children of the bridechamber fast, while the bridegroom is with them? As long as they have the bridegroom with them, they cannot fast. But the days will come when the bridegroom shall be taken away from them, and then shall they fast in those days' (Mark 2:19–20; cf. Matthew 9:14–15; Luke 5:33–35). In these gospel references one finds the symbolism of the messianic bridegroom and the messianic wedding, but no explicit mention of the bride. The same is true of the parable of the wise and foolish virgins: the bridegroom tarries, and when at midnight the cry is heard, 'Behold, the bridegroom cometh; go ye out to meet him,' the five foolish virgin-attendants find that they are unprepared and the door to the wedding is shut against them (Matthew 25:1–13). The parable seems to assume a familiarity with the analogy of the Parousia to a wedding banquet, implied in another Matthean parable, the invitation to the wedding banquet (22:1–14; cf. St John Chrysostom, *Homily on Matthew,* 69), and is explicit in the symbolism of the marriage of the

Lamb in Revelation 19:9. Thus, in the New Testament we find a fusion of two eschatological images of late biblical and intertestamental Judaism: the messianic banquet and the messianic marriage.

The Apocalypse presents a composite version of the foregoing biblical nuptial imagery in the context of the climactic eschatological battle between good and evil built around three contrasting pairs of characters: God, Christ, and the Bride on one side, and Satan, the Antichrist, and the Harlot on the other. Early Christian commentators regularly identified the Bride of chapters 19–22 (and the Lady of chapter 12) as the church, while medieval and subsequent Catholic expositors (e.g., William of Newburgh) often favoured a more specifically Marian reading. Especially influential in Christian symbolism was the description of the heavenly Jerusalem as the Bride of Christ (Revelation 21:2, 9), and the concluding words of the book, and of the New Testament, in which 'the Spirit and the bride say, Come,' and the evangelist echoes with the prayer, 'Even so, come, Lord Jesus'. Commentators frequently paralleled these words with the love-invitation of the Song of Solomon – and indeed, taken together, the Song of Solomon and the Apocalypse have been the key texts for the subsequent elaboration of Christian bride / bridegroom symbolism.

Given this biblical imagery, it is not surprising that the Church Fathers could view the life of Christ as a whole, from incarnation to resurrection, in terms of the nuptial allegory, as St Augustine expresses in a single sentence: 'If a man should give his own blood for his bride, he would not live to take her for his wife. But our Lord, dying without fear, gave his blood for her (the church) whom he was to obtain at his resurrection, and whom he had united to himself in the Virgin's womb' (In Joannis Evangelium Tractatus 8, Patrologia Latina, 35.1452). Even more prominent was the elaboration of the image of the church as Bride of Christ, as in such early Christian writings as St Methodius' Symposium (see especially 'Thecla's Hymn') and the Shepherd of Hermas and, above all, in Christian allegorizations of the Song of Solomon beginning with the earliest commentators, St Hippolytus and Origen in the 3rd century, and extending through hundreds of commentaries and poetic paraphrases from medieval to modern times, especially in monastic circles, notable examples including the commentaries of St Gregory of Nyssa, St Gregory the Great,

St Bernard, William of St Thierry, Gilbert of Hoyland, St
Cross, and, among Reformers, Beza, Luther, and John (
such influential poetic paraphrases as the Cantica section or reter
Riga's *Aurora,* William's *Expositio in Cantica Canticorum* with its Old
High German gloss, and the Song of Solomon section of Macé de la
Charité's French versification of the Bible or the 12th-century French
paraphrase in Le Mans Manuscript 173 (ed. Pickford, 1974). Dante
uses the imagery when in the Earthly Paradise Beatrice is called to
heaven with the words of Song of Solomon 4:8, *'Veni sponsa, de
Libano'* (*Purgatorio,* 30.11), and Dante calls Paradise itself a wedding
(*Paradiso,* 30.135) and the Church Triumphant Christ's spouse: 'In
form, then, of a white rose displayed itself to me that sacred soldiery
which in his blood Christ made his spouse' (*Paradiso,* 31.1–3).

The application of this nuptial imagery to the life of the church
had from earliest times special reference to the liturgy and the
sacraments. The early ritual for the dedication of a church, for instance,
emphasized the Bride of Christ figure, as is reflected in the 6th-century
hymn *'Urbi Beate Hierusalem'* and later adaptations such as the
sequences of Adam of St Victor. More centrally, the sacraments of
Eucharist and baptism, especially in the context of the Paschal liturgy of
the Easter Vigil (traditional setting in the West for the ritual of Christian
Initiation for adults) are given nuptial overtones in the basic early
Christian texts. About the Eucharist Theodoret says, 'In eating the
elements of the Bridegroom and drinking His Blood, we accomplish a
marriage union' (*Patrologia Graeca,* 81.1285), an image incorporated
into various Eastern liturgies. Similarly, the important catechetical
addresses by St Cyril of Jerusalem (*Procatechesis* and *Catechesis*) and St
Ambrose (*De mysteriis* and *De sacramentis*), directed to candidates for
baptism and the newly baptized, explicate the baptism ritual as a
'nuptial bath' and the Eucharist as a 'wedding banquet'. This symbolic
imagery is reflected in liturgical poetry and hymnody from St Ephraim
Syrus and Adam of St Victor to modern times.

It becomes a prominent motif in Edward Taylor's 'Preparatory
Meditations' in 17th-century New England, as in Keble's *The Christian
Year* in Victorian England. A familiar example in interdenominational
hymnals is S.J. Stone's well-known Protestant hymn 'The Church's
One Foundation':

> From heaven he came and sought her,
> To be his holy bride;
> With his own blood he bought her,
> And for her life he died.

In traditional Catholic doctrine the symbolic images applied to the church generally (*generaliter*) applied with special force (*specialiter*) to the Virgin Mary, as paradigm of the church; thus the Mother of God became also, paradoxically, the Bride of Christ. Evidence from early liturgies (Mozarabic, Gallican) indicates that the original Marian feast included celebration of her role as Queen of heaven's King, through application of the epithalamial Psalm 44. By the 7th century the Roman rite recognized four Marian feasts (Purification, Annunciation, Assumption, and Nativity of Mary), and in the 13th and 14th centuries the number of Marian feasts multiplied greatly and with regional variants; the Masses for these feasts, especially for the Assumption, all contained lections, such as selections from the Song of Solomon, which imply the nuptial metaphor. This symbolism is more fully developed in the monastic offices for these same feasts, as can be seen in such examples from the medieval English church as the Durham Collectar, the Leofric Collectar, the York Breviary, or a Sarum Missal from about 1300 (ed. Legg, 1916, 308–09). A particularly rich example is the office developed by nuns of the Brigittine order at Isleworth, who also produced an English translation and commentary, *The Myroure of oure Ladye,* printed in 1530 (Early English Text Society extra series 19). The hymns and prayers of the hours for each day of the week in *The Myroure* consistently make use of nuptial symbolism, as in the Thursday compline hymn 'Sponsa Iungende,' and its commentary, which claims that St Bridget herself was told by God the Father to tell 'that preste my louer that he make that hympne... to stande as hathe sette yt. For whyle holy cherche calleth all sowles the spouses of my sonne, moche more maye the sowle of Mary be called hys spowse' (page 238). It is above all in the office for Saturday, Mary's day, devoted to her life from the Passion to the Assumption, that this symbolism is most elaborated.

Further evidence of the Marian application of nuptial symbolism occurs in the homiletic literature and hymnody associated with the Marian feasts, especially the Assumption, in the Middle Ages. A good example is the collection of eight Marian homilies of Amedeus of Lausanne, especially the third (on the Assumption) and sixth (on Mary's joy in the Resurrection), in which the nuptial symbol supplies the central motif and concluding peroration. Similarly, the Blickling homily for the Annunciation speaks of Gabriel as announcing a wedding, and Mary's womb as a bridechamber in which the spiritual marriage between Christ and humanity is accomplished – though, once again, Mary herself is also the bride (Early English Text Society old series 58, pages 2–13). Another Old English example is Aelfric's first Assumption homily (based on the Pseudo-Jerome *Epistle 9*, '*Cogitis Me*', *Patrologia Latina*, 30.130), which applies the praises of the bride of the Song of Solomon to Mary in her glorification (ed. Thorpe, 1844, 1.436–54), as also does a Middle English homily on the Assumption following the Sarum rite (Early English Text Society old series 209, page 366).

Marian liturgical poetry makes similar use of such nuptial symbolism, as evidenced by Ephraim Syrus' Nativity Hymns and Adam of St Victor's sequences for Epiphany, such as '*De Beate Virgine,*' and the Nativity of Mary, such as '*Lux Advenit Veneranda*' (ed. Wrangham, 1881, nos 90, 95). Numerous similar examples may be garnered from among the poems collected in *Lateinische Hymnen des Mittelalters* (ed. F.J. Mone, 1964, 3 volumes) and *Analecta Hymnica Medii Aevi* (eds. Dreves and Blume, 1886, 55 volumes), such as '*Psalterium Beate Mariae Virgine,*' attributed to Edmund of Canterbury, in which Mary is repeatedly addressed, '*Ave, sponsa...*' (Dreves and Blume, volume 35, no. 10; cf. volume 9, nos 58, 60, and 61; and Mone, nos 326, 336, 371, 373, 447, 450, 469, 471, 473, 505, 510, 511, 515, 531, 555, and 600). The same motifs are discernible in medieval vernacular religious poetry – as in the use of the 'bryd' image in the Advent lyrics of the Exeter Book (ed. Campbell, 1959, 49, 67), the early Middle English 'On god ureisun of ure lefdi' (C. Brown, *English Lyrics of the XIIIth Century*, no. 3), the Lambeth Manuscript poem '*Gaude, Flore Virginali,*' whose second stanza begins, 'Gaude, goddys spouse so deere!' (Early English Text Society old series 15, pages 174–75), or the well-known '*Quia Amore Langueo,*' ending with Mary's invitation to the soul to participate with her in the spiritual marriage (Brown, *Religious Lyrics of the XIVth Century*, no. 132). The 15th century was the golden age of Middle English poetry of this sort, much of it modelled on the rhetoric of secular love lyrics, again using the precedent of the Song of Solomon, or the various versions of hymns on the Seven Heavenly Joys of the Virgin Mary, the second of which is her spousehood (ibid., nos 33–36; cf. nos 6, 14, 23, and 72). So exalted is this title, spouse of God, that one lyric (no. 69) does not shrink from naming her 'goddes,' being of 'One spyrte and will with cryst'.

Comparable to these Middle English productions, and with even more elaboration of this nuptial imagery, are the Marian poems of Heinrich von Frauenlob (died 1317), notably his impassioned 'Unser Frauen Lied' (see P. Wackernagel, ed., *Das Deutsche Kirchenlied von der altesten Zeit bis zu Anfang des XVII. Jahrhunderts*, 1867, 2.216–20). Here Mary's life is described allegorically under various images relating to the figure of Wisdom, the Lady of the Apocalypse, and the Bride of the Song of Solomon; in the second half she speaks in her own voice as the Bride, telling how her divine Lover came to her by night, kissed her, lay between her breasts, and entered – as an infant – her maiden womb, making her at once bride and mother (6–18, citing Song of Solomon 1:13), bringing about her nuptial 'deification' or interidentification with Christ:

> er got, si got, ich got: daz ich vor niemen spar.
> ich vater muter, er min muter vater zwar,
> wan daz ist war. (12.27–29)

The love-lyric analogy culminates in stanza 15, in which Mary portrays Christ and herself as a pair of lovers discovered by the Swain's angry Father, who 'punishes' him and casts him out of the kingdom; but by patiently bearing his suffering, the lover wins back the kingdom, to which he brings his spouse. This daring allegory is in fact comparable to other mystical representations of the spiritual marriage as a passionate love story, as in Thomas of Hales' 'Love Rune' (C. Brown, *English Lyrics of the XIIIth Century*, no. 43), the kingly wooer parable in *The Ancrene Riwle* (part 7), or St John of the Cross' poem 'Madrigal a lo divino,' in which the young lover, Christ, despised by his beloved, goes off to fight in foreign wars, until eventually he 'swarmed a tall tree and arms balancing wide / beautifully grappled the tree till he died / of the love in his heart like a ruinous wound' (trans. Nims, 1959, 41), or as in late medieval iconographic depictions of the Crucifixion showing Christ stabbed in the heart not by a Roman centurion but by the Sponsa herself.

As these latter references indicate, whatever is said of Mary *specialiter* becomes true of the church *generaliter* and of every faithful soul *individualiter* – and first of all in the case of certain female saints to whom the nuptial symbolism became particularly attached, notably Mary Magdalene and Katherine of Alexandria. The Mass and office of Mary Magdalene (July 22) is filled with nuptial references, especially to the bride's nocturnal search for her lover, which is applied to the Magdalene's Easter morning vigil, and the image appears in vernacular literary treatments, such as Robinson's *Life and Death of Mary Magdalene* (1620). But the saint most consistently identified as spouse of Christ is Katherine of Alexandria, the highborn patron of philosophy and learning who refused to take any husband other than Christ; the story of her martyrdom is highlighted by the account of her mystical marriage to Christ and at her death she is called by her divine Spouse to join him in heaven, in the words which conclude the Apocalypse: 'Come thou, my much beloved, come my bride!' The imagery occurs in the liturgy for Katherine (Nov. 25) and in the associated hymnody, such as Konrad von Heimburg's *'Ave Candens Lilium'* or Albert von Prag's *'Salve, Virgo Floriosa'* (Dreves and Blume, *Analecta Hymnica Medii Aevi*, volume 3, nos 56 and 20; cf. Mone, *Latinische Hymnen des Mittelalters*, nos 987, 989, 995, 997, 1000, and 1001), and in narrative accounts such as the late Old English *Life of St Katherine* (Early English Text Society old series 80) or John Capgrave's monumental poetic version of the 15th century (Early English Text Society old series 100). Capgrave's book 3 describes Katherine's conversion (baptism is her nuptial bath, 1069–73) and mystical marriage to Christ (1268–1309; subsequently, rejecting any repudiation of Christ, she dies a martyr for her spouse: 'I wil neuere chaunge, whil I haue lyf, / I shal been euere to hym truwe spouse and wyf' (4.1049–50). Subsequently, Katherine's mystical marriage became a favourite theme of Renaissance painters, such as Fra Angelico, Correggio, Luini, Raphael, Titian, Veronese, Tintoretto, and Murillo.

Just as mystical nuptial symbolism attached to certain specific saints (others include Catherine of Siena, Cecelia, Margaret, and Bridget), so it attached itself to female mystics and holy women generally in the late Middle Ages, and is reflected in the ritual for the investiture of nuns and in the rite for the Consecration of a Virgin. The background for these rites is found in early Christian texts dealing with the concept of virginity as dedication to spiritual marriage with Christ, such as Methodius' *Symposium,* Ambrose's treatises *De Virginitate, Exhortatio ad Virgines,* and *De Virginibus,* and Jerome's *Epistle 22* ('To Eustochium') and the influential *Adversus Jovinianum* (cited, e.g., by Chaucer's Wife of Bath – as an antifeminist diatribe), and such later medieval texts as *The Ancrene Riwle* (Early English Text Society old series 225, 249) and *Hali Meidenhad* (Early English Text Society old series 18). The theme is developed in the liturgies and offices for holy women (Common for a Virgin, Common for a Virgin Martyr, Common for a Holy Woman), especially in the repeated use of the Ambrosian hymn *'Jesu, Corona Virginum'*. The investiture of a nun and the rite for the Consecration of a Virgin are the liturgical culmination of the theme, being conceived according to the imagery of a wedding ceremony, including the donning of wedding garb and veil, bestowal of a ring, and the exchange of vows: 'My Lord Jesus Christ has espoused me with his ring and as a bride has adorned me with a crown'. A richly detailed explication of the Consecration Rite occurs in the third exercise of Gertrude the Great's *Exercises:* 'Espousals and Consecration of the Anniversary of Holy Profession' (trans. Gertrude Jaren Lewis and Jack Lewis, 1989). As the opening rubric explains: 'This is the way in which thou shalt solemnize the spiritual wedlock, the marriage of love, the betrothal, and the nuptials of thy chaste soul with Jesus the heavenly Bridegroom in the deathless bond of thy heart's affection,' for Christ is an impassioned Lover who 'loveth thee immoderately'.

While having special force in the context of female saints and the rituals of nuns and holy women, the nuptial metaphor was always understood to be applicable to every individual devout soul (as is evident in tropological commentaries on the Song of Solomon); consequently, it is a frequent image in the writings of the mystics, for whom it had great appeal. A striking instance is the lyrical treatise *The*

Flowing Light of Godhead by St Mechthild of Magdeburg, an associate of Gertrude the Great. Mechthild's book, widely circulated and translated (a 15th-century English version was entitled 'The Book of St Maud or Book of Ghostly Grace'), tells in loosely connected lyric sections the story of a divine Youth and the maiden he woos in a flowery meadow, their festive wedding, her apparent abandonment and inconsolable longing, and his reaffirmation and promise of everlasting union in the heavenly Garden of Love (*Revelations of Mechthild*, trans. Menzies, 1953). Her inconsolable sense of loss in this world is the inevitable condition of souls spiritually advanced, for nothing else can satisfy her – not the church, not the communion of saints, not even the adoration of the Christ-Child – for 'That is a childish love, to quiet children with. I am a full-grown bride and will have my Bridegroom.' The final mysteries of love are unutterable, as Soul explains to Understanding: 'No bride may tell what happens to her!' At last, she can only pray (in lines akin to those of Donne's 'Batter My Heart') to be vanquished by God.

A whole tradition of mystical literature similarly reflects this nuptial allegory, from Latin and vernacular poems such as Konrad's *'Epithalamium Christi Virginum Alternantium'* (Dreves and Blume, *Analecta Hymnica Medii Aevi*, volume 50, no. 343), or the many variants of Bernard's *'Dulcis Jesu Memoria'* (Dreves and Blume, *Ein Jahrtausend Lateinischer Hymnendichtung*, 1909, 2.35), or German *Geistliche minne*, such as the monumental 'nuptial epic,' *Christus und die Minnende Seele* (ed. Banz, 1908), to the classic works of systematic mysticism, such as Richard of St Victor's *Benjamin Minor* (book 5) and *The Four Degrees of Passionate Charity*, Hugh of St Victor's *The Soul's Betrothal-Gift*, Suso's *Love-Book* and *Little Book of Wisdom*, Lull's *Book of the Lover and the Beloved*, and the treatises on spiritual marriage by Gerson (*Spiritualibus Nuptiis*) and William of Ruysbroek (*The Adornment of the Spiritual Marriage*, ed. Underhill, 1916). Important examples in Middle English literature include the ascetic/contemplative treatise *The Wohunge of Ure Lauerd* and the poetic and prose pieces associated with it (Early English Text Society old series 241), and above all the works of Richard Rolle, especially *Incendium Amoris* and the various poems of love-longing and heart-wounding of the 'school of Rolle,' such as those of the Vernon Manuscript (Early English Text Society old series 98) or Camb.

Manuscript Dd. 5.64.III. In *The Pearl* the visionary maiden describes herself as a bride of the Lamb (757–59), one of those arrayed for the wedding in the heavenly Jerusalem (781–92).

The undisputed classics of nuptial spirituality are the poems and commentaries of the 16th-century Spanish mystics, especially John of the Cross' *Dark Night of the Soul, Spiritual Canticle,* and *Living Flame of Love* (each work taking the form of a commentary on a love poem of the same name), and St Teresa's *Interior Castle* (the sixth Mansion concerns Spiritual Betrothal, and the seventh, Spiritual Marriage) and *Conceptions of the Love of God.* Other examples include Luis de Leon's commentary on the Song of Solomon, and passages relating to the spiritual marriage theme in his *Names of Christ* (1921 edition, 2.217–19, 228–30, 236–38), as well as the Song of Solomon commentaries of Juan de los Angeles, Jeronimo Gracien, and Luis de la Puente. While most prominent in Catholic milieux, the theme also appears among radical and Anabaptist writers of the Reformation (e.g., Melchior Hofmann's 'The Ordinances of God' or the Letters of Samuel Rutherford) and also in mainstream Protestant literature, but usually with an emphasis on the corporate church rather than on the contemplative soul as Bride of Christ – as in the Song of Solomon commentaries of Beza, Luther, John Cotton, James Durham, and Joseph Hall or the biblical annotations of the Geneva Bible, the Synod of Dort, or the Westminster Assembly (1645), or in such occasional references as John Winthrop's use of the Bride / church metaphor in his 1645 'Speech to the General Court' (Miller, *The American Puritans*, 1982, 93).

In English poetry other than the Middle English religious lyrics discussed above, bride / bridegroom symbolism occurs in a diversity of contexts. Chaucer's Parson alludes to the image of a chaste virgin as a 'spouse to Jhesu Crist' (*Parson's Tale*, 10.947), but Chaucer's other references are in the vein of moral satire. Whereas the significance of the erotic imagery derived from the Song of Solomon in goliardic Latin love lyrics remains a matter of critical dispute (i.e., whether such poems as *'Iam Dulcis Amica'* or *'Veni Delectissime'* of the Cambridge MS, or the love songs of the *Carmina Burana,* are composed in the spirit of romantic elevation of carnal love or of irreverent bawdy parody or yet again of moral satire), it is clear that the parodies of the Song of Solomon in the mouths of Absolon (*Miller's Tale*, 1.3698–707) and

January (*Merchant's Tale*, 4.2138–48) are ironic devices used to heighten the moral disparity between Chaucer's lewd and grotesque pairs of lovers, on the one hand, and Christ and Mary, his spouse, on the other. Similarly, in the *Roman de la Rose* echoes of the Song of Solomon reinforce a pattern of moral satire in which the *hortus deliciarum* of Amant contrasts with the Garden of the Good Shepherd, and Genius' advice to men to labour assiduously at copulation and Amant's final rape of the Rose serve as a brutal satiric parody of the idea of spiritual marriage. In the *Book of the Duchess,* on the other hand, the description of Blanche in terms of the Bride of the Song of Solomon (895–984) seems to be part of a 'Boethian' awakening on the part of the sorrowful knight as he comes to recognize that what he really loves in the Duchess is beyond death and time.

In a similar vein Renaissance epithalamia and other love poems could use biblical imagery to elevate their praise of a maiden through implied comparison to the heavenly Bride and Groom, as in Spenser's 'Epithalamium' (167–84) and *Amoretti* (nos 15, 64, 77) or the descriptions of noble women in the *Faerie Queene* (1.12.21–22, Una; 2.3.22–29, Belphoebe; 6.8.42, Serena), whose heavenly archetype appears in Spenser's description of Sapience in 'An Hymne of Heavenly Beautie' (183ff.). In the emblem book tradition, books 4 and 5 of Quarles' *Emblems* (1635) contain love lyrics of the soul enamoured of the Divine Lover, Van Veen's *Amoris Divini Emblemata* (1660) features engravings of a winged Amor Divinis and the beloved Anima, along with verses in Dutch and French, while Hugo's *Pia Desideria,* Englished by Arwaker (1686), similarly presents images of the allegorical pair of lovers. Related to these are the numerous poetic paraphrases of the Song of Solomon in Renaissance poetry, such as Drayton's *Harmonie of the Church* (1591), Wither's *Hymns and Songs of the Church* (1623), Quarles' *Sions Sonnets* (1625), or Isaac Watts' *Hymns and Spiritual Songs* (1707–48, nos 67–68).

Donne refers to the church / Bride figure in 'Upon the Annunciation and Passion falling upon one day,' noting that, as God has joined creation and judgment, death and conception, so the liturgical calendar of the church, 'his imitating Spouse,' occasionally celebrates Annunciation and Passion simultaneously. Donne devotes Holy Sonnet 18 ('Show me, dear Christ, thy Spouse') to the church /

Spouse metaphor, but adding the apparently paradoxical petition that Christ share his spouse with all –

> Betray kind husband thy spouse to our sights,
> And let myne amorous soule court thy mild Dove,
> Who is most trew, and pleasing to thee, then
> When she's embrac'd and open to most men

thus putting the soul in the unusual role of husband of the church. More conventionally, in the *Second Anniversary,* Donne speaks of the deceased Elizabeth as she who 'was here / Betroth'd to God, and now is married there' (462). The individual as spouse of God is implicit also in the more violent erotic paradoxes of the concluding sestet of Holy Sonnet 14, 'Batter My Heart'. Herbert calls the church Christ's Spouse in 'The Church Militant' (9–13), and in 'Sunday' describes the Sundays of a person's life, threaded on time's string, as bracelets that 'adorn the wife / Of the eternall glorious King'. Additionally, 'Longing' is a love poem addressed to God in the manner of Rolle's songs of love-longing. Vaughan frequently alludes to the nuptial metaphor in *Silex Scintillans,* e.g., in 'The Search' (64), 'Faith' (5), 'The Dawning' (2), 'The World' (5, 59), 'The Constellation' (57), 'The Knot' (1), and 'L'Envoy' (33).

In Crashaw's poetry the spousal imagery is associated primarily with poems about female saints or addressed to religious women. 'The Hymn in the Assumption' makes the conventional association of Mary with the Bride of the Song of Solomon; the 'Third elegie' of the Alexias series ends with an account of the life of St Cecilia as a bride of Christ; and, most dramatically, 'A Hymne to Sainte Teresa' hails her as a spouse of Christ, especially in the image of the transverberation or piercing of her heart by a seraphic angel with 'a Dart thrice dip't in that rich flame / Which writes the spouse's radiant Name' (81–82), and the final movement of 'The Flaming Heart' (69–108), which is wholly premised on the image of Teresa as Christ's enraptured bride. Crashaw also applies the image in a series of poems urging religious women to take Christ as their spiritual husband: 'A Letter to the Countess of Denbigh,' 'To [Mrs M.R.] Councel concerning her Choice,' and especially 'Ode on a Prayer-Book,' the second half of which is an unrestrained panegyric on the

> Amorous languishments, luminous trances… Delicious
> Deaths, soft exhalations
> Of soul; dear and divine annihilations…
>> Which the divine embraces
> Of the deare spouse of spirits with them will bring.
> (70–84)

concluding

> Happy proof! she shall discover,
>> What joy, what bliss,
>> How many heavens at once it is,
> To have a God become her Lover! (121–24)

After the 17th century, the biblical metaphor of spiritual marriage becomes less common outside strictly church-related literature. Variants of the symbolism appear among the Romantic poets, as in Blake's image of *The Marriage of Heaven and Hell* as a mystical 'coincidential oppositorum'. Jung, in *Mysterium Coniunctionis,* traces the whole history of such mystical marriage symbolism in gnostic, hermetic, and alchemical texts, and relates it to his anima / animus theory of the psyche; and much Romantic poetry, such as Shelley's 'Epipsychidion,' his spousal song to his divine anima, could be read in this context. In a different vein, Coleridge in 'Dejection' speaks of the wedding of nature and the imagination: 'And in our life alone does Nature live: / Ours is her wedding garment, ours her shroud!' (49–50). Wordsworth, in 'Home at Grasmere,' similarly posits the wedding of 'the discerning intellect of Man… to this goodly universe,' and tells how in a prophetic mode he 'Would chant, in lonely peace, the spousal verse / Of this great consummation' (52–58), symbolism fulfilled in the climactic Mount Snowdon episode in book 14 of *The Prelude.*

The more conventional church as spouse symbol does continue to appear, as in some passing references in Browning's *The Ring and the Book* (6.961–65; 7.446–49; 8.694–96; 10.1484–86; 11.1297–1300), where the reference is used variously to refer to the archetypal standard of either marriage or the priesthood, or in some passages of dialogue in Tennyson's plays, e.g., *Queen Mary* (3.3.205; 4.199) and *Becket* (5.2.22 and 3.3.174–75, where Becket uses the image to proclaim the plight of the English church: 'Ay, King! for in thy kingdom, as thou knowest, / The spouse of the Great King, thy King, hath fallen'). In 'St Agnes' Eve' Tennyson recounts the prayer of a nun longing to be drawn up to the heavens to be reunited with her heavenly spouse, ending with her vision of an eternal Sabbath, 'A light upon the shining sea – / The Bridegroom with his bride!' Conventional nuptial imagery is used in Keble's *The Christian Year* in the hymns for the Second Sunday after Epiphany, Sexagesima Sunday, St Matthias Day, Holy Communion, the Visitation and Communion of the Sick, Commination, and for the Gunpowder Treason (in which he speaks of 'The Widow'd Church... the lonely Spouse'). In 'The Starlight Night' Gerard Manley Hopkins concludes his sacramental meditation with the words, 'This piece-bright paling shuts the spouse / Christ home, Christ and his mother and all his hallows,' and his 'Habit of Perfection' incorporates the Franciscan-inspired image of holy Poverty as a bride.

Other writers have approached the spiritual marriage symbolism in a satirical or ironic mode, as in the many gothic novels utilizing a monastic setting in a lurid manner such as M.G. Lewis' *The Monk,* or Huxley's *The Devils of Verdun;* or they have approached it with ambiguity, as in the case of Pielmeier's *Agnes of God;* or from the point of view of neocabalistic symbolism, as in the case of Nathaniel Tarn's epic poem *Lyrics for the Bride of God* (1970). Finally among contemporary writers, several poems by William Everson (Brother Antoninus) in *The Veritable Years* revive the imagery of spiritual eroticism, as in 'The Encounter' or 'The Song the Body Dreamed in the Spirit's Mad Behest,' which begins, 'Call Him the Lover and call me the Bride,' and goes on to recount a violent ravishing of Flesh by Spirit:

> Folding Him in the chaos of my loins
> I pierce through armies tossed upon my breast,
> Envelop in love's tidal dredge of faith
> His huge unrest.

Everson's 'River-Root / A Syzygy' parallels the rising of a river and a married couple's sexual conjunction as an incarnational participation in the cosmic mystery of union. Another example of erotic nature-mysticism is the opening passage of Annie Dillard's *Holy the Firm,* in which the author describes her moment of waking as a spiritual betrothal:

> I wake in a god. I wake in arms holding my quilt,
> holding me as best they can inside my quilt
> Someone is kissing me – already. I wake, I cry 'Oh,'
> I rise from the pillow. Why should I open my eyes?
> I open my eyes. The god lifts from the water...
> Today's god rises, his long eyes flecked in clouds. He flings
> his arms, spreading colours; he arches, cupping sky in his
> belly; he vaults, vaulting and spread,
> holding all and spread on me like skin.

George L. Scheper
Essex Community College
and Johns Hopkins University School of Continuing Study

Hortus Conclusus

The only direct biblical reference, albeit a metaphorical one, to a *hortus conclusus* or enclosed garden is Song of Solomon 4:12: 'my spouse is an enclosed garden.' However, the orchards of Song 4:13 and Ecclesiastes 2:5 and the 'King's forest' of Nehemiah 2:8 also denote enclosed parks or pleasure gardens similar to Cyrus' garden at Ceaenae (Xenophon, *Anabasis,* 1.2.7), Solomon's garden (Josephus, *Antiquities,* 8.7), the king's garden near Siloam (Nehemiah 3:15), or the vivaria described by Aulus Gellius (*Noctes Atticae,* 2.20.4). Designated by the Hebrew word *pardes,* which occurs in the Old Testament in only the three instances cited above, such grounds are perhaps related to the Old Persian *pairidaeza,* meaning an enclosed park, and should be distinguished etymologically from the Garden of Eden of Genesis 2:8. In the Septuagint translation of the Pentateuch, the Greek term *paradeisos* is used to refer not only to the Garden of Eden but also to render the Hebrew word *pardes.* Thus through Greek translation all gardens are semantically linked to the Garden of Eden.

The primal Paradise of the Old Testament is a distinct geographical location, but in the New Testament its meaning is extended to the celestial paradise, as in Luke 23:43. A merging of the concepts of earthly and heavenly paradise occurs frequently in later apocalyptic and rabbinic commentaries, especially after the Hebrew word *pardes* had been influenced by its Greek cognate *paradeisos*.

Some midrashic interpretation of the allusion to the bride as an enclosed garden has construed it as a reference to the confinement of the Hebrews in Egypt, thus treating it as part of the commentary on Exodus. Comparable Christian interpretation holds that the enclosed garden signifies the church, which contains only the faithful. (Such a view persists until after the Reformation, as in Isaac Watts' hymn 'We are a Garden Walled Around'.) The lines of Song of Solomon 5:4–5 ('My beloved put in his hand by the hole of the door, and my bowels were moved for him. I arose up to open to my beloved; and my hands dropped with myrrh, and my fingers with sweet smelling myrrh, upon the handles of the lock') were interpreted as a chaste allegory of Christ knocking at the door of the world and appealing to the faithful. Similarly, 7:7–8 ('This thy stature is like to a palm tree, and thy breasts to clusters of grapes. I said, I will go up to the palm tree, I will take hold of the boughs thereof') was taken to mean that Christ would cling to his church and prevent its branches from being shaken by winds of heresy. In developing Christian exegesis of the Song of Solomon, the bride came also to represent both the individual soul wooed by God and the Virgin Mary.

In medieval literature the image of the virgin as a locked garden became intermingled with the motif of classical gardens of love, a factor in the tradition of courtly love in which the lover had to undergo certain trials before he could win the chaste love of his lady. Such a pattern is exemplified in *Roman de la Rose* and in Chaucer's *Parliament of Fowls*; it is memorably parodied in Chaucer's *Merchant's Tale*. Claudian's *Epithalamion for Honorius Augustus* offers perhaps the most elaborate description of the classical *hortus conclusus* as the abode of Venus, and his legacy to the Middle Ages was, according to Giamatti (*The Earthly Paradise and the Renaissance Epic*, 252), 'to fix firmly the conventions of a natural bower or grove or enclosure dedicated to Venus and her pastimes'. Once Claudian's garden of Venus was transferred into a Christian context, it was fused with allegorized treatments of the enclosed garden of Song of Solomon to produce the religious symbol of the Virgin Mary in her *hortus conclusus.* A complicated iconographical scheme for representing the incarnation in this way appears in many paintings and tapestries, e.g., the Dame à la Licorne in the Cluny Museum or the Annunciation of Domenico Veneziano.

The enclosed garden acquired its most potent connotations from its association with Eden and hence its connection with visions of earthly paradise. Such visions, particularly in the Renaissance, were nourished by myths of the Golden Age, Elysium, and the Isles of the Blest found in Hesiod, Homer, Ovid, Pindar, and Virgil. For Christian commentators such pagan fables were understood to be dim, sometimes distorted versions of the true paradise of Eden, a link made by Thomas Burnet in his *Sacred Theory of the World*. Milton ransacked classical legends to adumbrate the qualities of the true Paradise in *Paradise Lost*. His Eden is more delightful than the 'feigned' gardens of Adonis or Alcinous, or even the actual garden of Song of Solomon, where Solomon, the 'sapient king,' dallied with his 'fair Egyptian spouse' (9.440–43). Milton's Eden also recalls the Golden Age sites of antiquity where there is perpetual spring and the Christian Latin paradises whose atmosphere is laden with fragrant breezes. Following Horace's *Epode 16*, it is also a peaceable kingdom, a 'Heaven on earth,' and a *hortus conclusus*, an 'enclosure wild,' a 'narrow room wherein Nature's whole wealth' is confined (4.207), surrounded by a 'verdurous wall' (4.143) from whose eastern gate Adam and Eve are expelled. Spenser's Garden of Adonis also belongs in the literary tradition of earthly paradises which include Homer's Garden of Alcinous (*Odyssey*, 7.112–34), Claudian's Cyprus garden in his Epithalamion, Dante's Eden in *Purgatorio* (28.138–40), and the Garden of Nature in Chaucer's *Parliament of Fowls* (120–308). It is linked with Eden, and in describing its weather as a 'continuall spring,' Spenser follows medieval and Renaissance literary models in offering the garden as a metaphor for the ideal world.

Certain common features of the earthly paradise emerged from the conflation of classical and biblical sources. Menelaus (*Odyssey*, book 4) learns of the 'Elysian plain at the world's end... where living is made easiest for mankind, where no snow falls, no strong winds, or rain.' This eternally balmy weather recurs in Ovid's *Metamorphoses* (book 1) in Claudian's garden of Venus, in the Christian paradise in

De ave phoenice attributed to Lactantius, in *De judicio Domini* ascribed to Tertullian, and in the Old English *Phoenix* of Cynewulf. The unchanging, innocent, and protected state of these paradises reappears in the latter-day Edens of Dickens' Dingley Dell and the gardens of P.G. Wodehouse's Blandings Castle.

For certain 17th-century writers such as Henry Hawkins in *Partheneia sacra* the enclosed garden remained a specific religious emblem to be distinguished from the Hesperides, the garden of Tempe, the Elysian fields, and the earthly Paradise. Gradually during the 17th century the 'analogic reading of nature' surrendered 'to more empirical appreciation'; thus Ralph Austen's *A Treatise of Fruit Trees* contains not only an emblem in which Solomon's praise of his bride as a *hortus conclusus* encircles a garden, but a geometrical plan for planting and a collection of tools for grafting and pruning.

In the 18th century, the image of Eden as a specific place devolved into mere literary allusion. In *Windsor Forest*, Pope writes: 'The Groves of Eden, vanished now so long, / Live in description, and look green in song' (7–8). And in his *Essay on Man*, he appeals to a more suitable source of inspiration, projecting the image of his Twickenham estate onto the universe: 'A mighty maze! but not without a plan; / A wild, where weeds and flowers promiscuous shoot, / Or garden tempting with forbidden fruit...' Despite Romantic enthusiasm for nature, 'Paradise, and groves / Elysian' were for Wordsworth 'a history of departed things'; in the *Prospectus to the Recluse*, he relocates paradise as a property of the human intellect.

Michael Goldberg
University of British Columbia

Love Strong as Death

Song of Solomon 8:6 reads: 'For love is strong as death; jealousy is as cruel as the grave: the coals thereof are coals of fire; which had a most vehement flame.' In English literary tradition the phrase is often conjured up ironically in connection with Shakespeare's *Romeo and Juliet* (e.g., Lynd, 'It's a Fine World'). In Christina Rossetti's *An End*, 'Love, strong as Death, is dead. / Come, let us make his bed / Among

the dying flowers.' The symbiosis of love and death undergirds Oscar
Wilde's 'The Canterville Ghost,' in which it is said, 'You can open for
me the portals of Death's house, for Love is always with you, and Love
is stronger than Death is.' Dorothy Sayers' Miss Chimpson, in
Unnatural Death, opines: 'The longer I live, my dear, the more certain
I become that jealousy is the most fatal of feelings. The Bible calls it
"cruel as the grave", and I'm sure that it is so. Absolute loyalty,
without jealousy, is the essential thing' (chapter 16).

David L. Jeffrey
University of Ottawa

Many Waters Cannot Quench Love

Song of Solomon 8:7 reads 'Many waters cannot quench love, neither
can the floods drown it.' Thomas Hardy borrows these words to
describe a love more complete than mere erotic attraction in *Far from
the Madding Crowd*: 'Where, however, happy circumstances permit its
development, the compounded feeling proves itself to be the only
love which is as strong as death – that love which many waters cannot
quench, nor the floods drown, beside which the passion usually
called by the name is evanescent as steam' (chapter 56).

David L. Jeffrey
University of Ottawa

Pomegranate

The pomegranate, called in Hebrew *rimmon* (Akkadian *armanna;*
Arabic *rumman*), is mentioned in the Old Testament in a variety of
contexts. Among the extended praises of the beloved in the Song of
Solomon is the comparison, 'thy temples are like a piece of
pomegranate within thy locks' (4:3; repeated at 6:7). Elsewhere, the
maiden in the Song declares, 'I would cause thee to drink of spiced
wine of the juice of my pomegranate' (8:2).

The pomegranate was not only a source of lyrical comparisons
but an erotic symbol as well, as is clearly seen in the well-known

hortus conclusus passage: 'A garden inclosed is my sister, my spouse; a spring shut up, a fountain sealed. Thy plants are an orchard of pomegranates, with pleasant fruits; camphire, with spikenard' (Song of Solomon 4:12–13). The pomegranate was traditionally a sign and symbol of fertility in the Near East, its budding presence a sign of a fertile land and the fruit itself, closely packed with seeds, a symbol of fertility, as in Song of Solomon 6:11: 'I went down into the garden of nuts, to see the fruits of the valley, to see whether the vine flourished, and the pomegranates budded' (cf. Song of Solomon 7:12).

The pomegranate is an important element in the identification of the Promised Land (Deuteronomy 8:8); indeed, the spies sent out to scout Canaan brought back with them as signs of the fertility and bounty of the land bunches of figs, grapes, and pomegranates (Numbers 13:23). Conversely, the absence of pomegranates is a sign of the absence of God's favour (Numbers 20:5; Joel 1:12; Haggai 2:19). This association accounts for the later legendary identification of the pomegranate with the tree of life, seen also in Christian iconography, as in the seventh tapestry in the series of Unicorn Tapestries at the Cloisters (New York).

The pomegranate is also used as a cultic/liturgical symbol in the Old Testament. The hem of the robe of the high priest was to be decorated with an alternation of golden bells and pomegranates of blue, purple, and scarlet (Exodus 28:33–34; 39:24–25; Ecclesiasticus 45:9). Exodus 28:35 implies that the sound the priest would make upon entering the sanctuary would be a kind of cultic warning, but some modern commentators have proposed that the 'bells' were originally representations of pomegranate flowers, to alternate with images of the fruit. Similarly, the temple of Solomon included columns of brass whose capitals were carved with images of pomegranates (1 Kings 7:18, 20, 42; 2 Chronicles 3:16; 4:13; also 2 Kings 25:17; Jeremiah 52:22).

In Jewish exegesis, the pomegranate is interpreted allegorically as symbolizing spiritual fertility, as in young scholars or rulers full of precepts or good works (Targum Ketubim, Song of Solomon 4:3, 13; 6:11; 7:12; cf. Midrash Rabba on the same passages). The pomegranates budding are interpreted as 'the children who are busy learning the Torah and sit in rows like pomegranate seeds' (Midrash

Rabba, Song of Solomon 6:11), and the garden of pomegranates as an image of the messianic age (Midrash Rabba, Song of Solomon 4:13).

Christian allegorists, likewise, used the pomegranate to signify spiritual fruitfulness in the church and the individual soul. The redness of the pomegranate rind and seeds was generally taken to refer to the church's imitation of Christ's passion through actual martyrdom or the spiritual martyrdom of the austere monastic life, while the whiteness of the pith symbolized virginity or purity.

The Old English word for pomegranate was *aeppel-cyrnel,* 'kernel-apple,' which became 'appel-garnade' in Middle English. The more familiar term *pome-sarnet-tys* occurs in Chaucer's translation, *The Romaunt of the Rose* (1355–58), as part of the description of the Garden of Love, a false 'paradise' which parodies the spiritual garden of Christian exegesis.

There are several incidental allusions to the pomegranate in Shakespeare (*All's Well That Ends Well*, 2.3.276 and *1 Henry 4*, 2.4.42) and one reference (*Romeo and Juliet*, 3.5.1–7, 11) which strongly recalls its erotic – and thanatopic – associations. Keats may be echoing Shakespeare in his 'Faery Song 1,' where the pomegranate retains its age-old connotation as the paradisal tree of life:

> Shed no tear – O shed no tear!...
> For I was taught in Paradise
> To ease my breast of melodies –
>   Shed no tear.
>
> Overhead – look overhead
> 'Mong the blossoms white and red –
> Look up, look up – I flutter now
> On this flush pomegranate bough. (1, 6–12)

In Canto 3 of *Don Juan* Byron uses the pomegranate image as part of the idyllic pastoral setting for the love of Juan and Haidee, 'happy in the illicit / Indulgence of their innocent desires' (3.13.1–8; cf. 3.62.6–8; 3.33.1–6).

The Song of Solomon, with its pomegranate image, is echoed also in Blake's prophetic poem *Ahania,* where Ahania, a personification of desire, longs for her lost mate, Urizen (reason or law):

'And when he gave my happy soul
To the sons of eternal joy;
When he took the daughters of life
Into my chambers of love...

'Swell'd with ripeness & fat with fatness,
Bursting on winds, my odours,
My ripe figs and rich pomegranates
In infant joy at thy feet,
O Urizen, sported and sang.

'Then thou with thy lap full of seed,
With thy hand full of generous fire,
Walked forth from the clouds of morning,
On the virgins of springing joy,
On the human soul to cast
The seed of eternal science...' (5.9, 11–12)

In Joyce's *Ulysses,* Leopold Bloom cites Song of Solomon 4:3 in his conversation with Stephen wherein 'fragments of verse from the ancient Hebrew and ancient Irish languages were cited with modulations of voice and translation of texts by guest to host and by host to guest': *'Kifeloch harimon rakatejch m'baad l'zamatejch'* ('thy temple amid thy hair is as a slice of pomegranate'). Hopkins, in his *Meditations on 'Spiritual Exercises',* explicates the pomegranate as a symbol of the prelapsarian plenitude and wholeness of all creation and of each kind and individual:

'Magnam capacitatem et ambitum mundi' – this suggests that 'pomegranate,' that *pomum possibilium.* The Trinity saw it whole and in every 'cleave,' the actual and the possible. We may consider that we are looking at it in all the actual cleaves, one after another. This sphere is set off against the sphere of the divine being, a steady 'seat or throne' of majesty. Yet that too has its cleave to us, the entrance of Christ on the world. There is not only the pomegranate of the whole world but of each species in it, each race, each individual, and so on. Of human nature the whole pomegranate fell in Adam (August 26, 1885; *Sermons and Devotional Writings,* ed. Devlin, 1959, 171).

No major poet seems to have been more fascinated by the

pomegranate or to have made more persistent use of it than Robert Browning, for whom it was a powerful emblem of the loving heart. In *Sordello* (1840), Palma's lyric effusion in which she confesses her love for Sordello is filled with rich nature imagery, culminating with the pomegranate (3.344–59). In 1841, Browning inaugurated a series of pamphlets as the vehicle for the publication of his poetry, the general title of which was *Bells and Pomegranates*. The first number was *Pippa Passes*, and in the title work the pomegranate occurs again, somewhat obscurely, as an emblem of love and change of heart.

After six numbers of *Bells and Pomegranates* had been published, Elizabeth Barrett took public notice of Browning's poetry; in her poem 'Lady Geraldine's Courtship,' she pays tribute to Browning's poetry using the pomegranate image to compliment him. Browning himself used the pomegranate image again in *Bells and Pomegranates* number 7, *Dramatic Romances and Lyrics* (November 1845), in the poem 'The Englishman in Italy'.

The following year, after repeated requests, he reluctantly agreed to give a public explanation of the meaning of the title of his series. In the eighth and last number of *Bells and Pomegranates* (April 1846), as a preface to *A Soul's Tragedy*, he wrote that

> I only meant by that title to indicate an endeavour towards something like an alternation, or mixture, of music with discoursing, sound with sense, poetry with thought; which looks too ambitious, thus expressed, so the symbol was preferred. It is little to the purpose that such is actually one of the most familiar of the many Rabbinical (and Patristic) acceptations of the phrase.

'Bells' was thus intended to convey the musical or sound element of his poetry, while 'pomegranates' represented the sense, what a medieval writer would call the 'doctrine'. That bells and pomegranates adorned the hem of the Old Testament high priest was also suggestive for Browning, who, like many of his contemporaries, attributed a priestly function to poetry.

George L. Scheper
Essex Community College and
Johns Hopkins University School of Continuing Study

Quia Amore Langueo

These words form the refrain of two of the best-known and most beautiful of Middle English lyrics. They come from the Song of Solomon (5:8, Vulgate), the King James Version translation of which reads somewhat confusingly, 'I charge you, O daughters of Jerusalem, if ye find my beloved, that ye tell him, that I am sick of love' (Vulgate 'I languish with love').

In the allegorical interpretation of the earlier Middle Ages (as represented by Cassiodorus, Bede, and St Gregory the Great), the love-longing is understood in connection with intercessory prayer or the promptings or conviction of the Spirit, and the speaker is seen as representing the human soul. In the writings of the Cistercians, especially St Bernard of Clairvaux, the Bride-speaker is identified also with the Virgin Mary. Hence, one Middle English adaption, probably to be associated with the Feast of the Assumption of the Virgin (August 15), begins:

> In a tabernacle of a toure,
> As I stode musyng on the mone,
> A crouned quene, most of honoure,
> Apered in gostly syght ful sone.
> (C. Brown, *Religious Lyrics of the XIVth Century*, number 132)

The Virgin is interceding, languishing on account of the 'loue of man my brother'. She urges the reader to look upon her as a 'sister and spouse'.

Another version (ed. Furnivall, Early English Text Society old series 15) presents the speaker discovering 'a man' (Christ) sitting under a tree upon a hill, wounded from head to foot, bleeding from the heart; the 'sistyr' for whom he longs is 'mannis soule'. This faithful lover, Christ, is found by one seeking 'in mounteyne and in mede, / Trustynge a trewe loue for to fynde'. The poem combines features of the Passion lyrics with appeals drawn from the whole vocabulary of love in the Song of Solomon.

An adaptation of Francis Quarles, more than a century later, concentrates on the 'daughters of Jerusalem,' which Quarles subtly identifies with the virgins of Jesus' parable about the coming of the

Bridegroom (Matthew 25:1–13). The speaker gives voice to the soul convicted by the Spirit:

> Deep wounded with the flames that furnaced from his eye.
> I charge you, virgins, as you hope to hear
> The heavenly music of your Lover's voice
> …tell him that a flaming dart
> Shot from his eye, hath pierced my bleeding heart,
> And I am sick of love, and languish in my smart.

David L. Jeffrey
University of Ottawa

Rose of Sharon

A reference to the bride of the Song of Solomon (2:1), the rose of Sharon becomes part of medieval typology of the Virgin Mary (e.g., in St Anthony of Padua and St Bernard of Clairvaux). Jonathan Edwards, in his *Personal Narrative,* says that the words represent to him 'the loveliness and beauty of Jesus Christ'; for Edward Taylor the phrase inspires a poem in his *Poems and Sacramental Meditations,* the 'Reflexion' to his first meditation, which compares the perfume of the rose to the sweetness of Christ's sacrifice celebrated in the Eucharist. In Sir Walter Scott's *Ivanhoe,* Prior Aymer agrees with her temporary captor that Rebecca is as beautiful as 'the very Bride of the Canticles,' indeed 'the Rose of Sharon and the Lily of the Valley,' then counters his licentious intentions with the parry 'but your Grace must remember that she is still but a Jewess' (chapter 7).

David L. Jeffrey
University of Ottawa

Solomon

Solomon was the third king of Israel (circa 961–922BC) and the second son of David (2 Samuel 12:18, 24). His kingdom, excluding Philistia and Phoenicia, stretched from Kadesh in the north to Ezion-geber in the south (1 Kings 4:21). Largely free from external threat, Solomon built extensively in Jerusalem, his best-known structure being the Temple. He strategically established fortified cities throughout the empire and negotiated trade agreements with other nations. On the Gulf of Aqabah and from Phoenicia, he developed maritime trade (9:26–28; 10:11, 22–29). But his legendary, wealthy reign (v. 23) bled the nation's resources, requiring heavy taxation and forced corvées (4:7; 5:13–14; 9:21).

Unlike Chronicles, which omits a negative assessment, 1 Kings traces Solomon's decline largely to religious syncretism provoked by marriage to 'many foreign women' (11:1–3). For these he built cultic sites and permitted worship of alien deities (vv. 7–8). The nation's strong unity faded under this influence (cf. Sirach 47:13–21).

Solomon's celebrated wisdom reportedly 'excelled the wisdom' of 'the east country, and all the wisdom of Egypt' (4:20–34). Notably illustrated in the episode with the two harlots (3:16–28) and the visit of the Queen of Sheba (10:1–29), this wisdom expressed itself in riddles and proverbs, as well as in extraordinary judicial acumen. Solomon's sagacity was sufficiently renowned that he was frequently credited with later canonical, apocryphal, and pseudepigraphal literature (e.g., the biblical 'wisdom' books as well as Wisdom of Solomon, Psalms of Solomon, Odes of Solomon, and Testament of Solomon). In the New Testament, Jesus mentions both Solomon's splendour (Matthew 6:29; Luke 12:27) and his wisdom (Matthew 12:42; Luke 11:31).

Jewish tradition assigns Solomon extensive knowledge of many subjects (Wisdom of Solomon 7:17–22). He is said to have authored works on medicine, mineralogy, and magic. Legends of Solomon's liaison with the Queen of Sheba (Balkis), also known in Arabic and Ethiopian versions, tell how Solomon married Balkis and gained control of Sheba. Arabic lore makes Solomon a devout follower of Allah and prototype of Mohammed. With the winds and demons at his disposal (Koran, *Sura* 21:82), he visits the Valley of the Ants (*Sura* 27:16–17) and the Queen of Sheba (vv. 20–45). One legend, resembling the *Arabian Nights,* has the jinn weave an enormous carpet on which Solomon goes on a hajj to Mecca, where he prophesies the birth of Mohammed.

In both Judaism and Christianity, the association of Solomon with demonology and magic flourished during late antiquity. According to the Testament of Solomon, Solomon received a magic ring seal from the archangel Michael with which to subjugate the demons and set them to building (1.5–7); Josephus connects magical seal rings with Solomon in an account of exorcism (*Antiquities*, 8.42–49). Scores of Jewish and Christian amulets and talismans invoke his power over demons. One amulet declares, 'Seal of Solomon, drive away all evil from him who wears [this]' (E.R. Goodenough, *Jewish Symbols*, 1953–68, 2.238). This notion of Solomon's power gives rise to the legend of his conquest of Asmodeus, the prince of demons, and his acquisition of the stonecutting *shamir*.

Patristic theology, on the other hand, focuses on Solomon's sagacity as a king and judge (cf. St Ambrose, *De fide*, book 1, prologue) and often portrays him as a type of Christ (cf. Ambrose, *De interpellatione Iob et David*, 4.4.15). Debate among the Fathers concerning whether Solomon repented his fall into luxury constitutes a tacit criticism of his wisdom, as does the medieval tale of Solomon's besting by Marcolphus the dullard and Morolf the dwarf.

While interest in Solomon as magician is strong in the Middle Ages – many books of magic, including the *Clavicula Salomonis*, are ascribed to him – he is, above all else, seen as a great moral teacher and leader. *The Ancrene Riwle* invokes him as an author of wise sayings (Camden Society, 1883, 64) who judges rightly (90). In Dante's *Paradiso*, the voice of St Thomas Aquinas introduces Solomon as the brightest of the twelve lights of philosophy (10.109–14), then argues for him as the model of kingly prudence (13.94–108). The fate of Solomon is the subject of speculation in *Piers Plowman*. In the 'C' text, Conscience uses the case of Solomon to argue that God's blessings can be withdrawn if the recipient proves unworthy (C.4.326–34) and concludes that Solomon is now in hell (see also B.12.266–74). The presence of Solomon the magician can be detected in Chaucer's *Squire's Tale* (*Canterbury Tales* 5.248–51). The successor of David appears elsewhere in *The Canterbury Tales* as 'he that so wel teche kan' (*Summoner's Tale*, 3.2085) and as 'the wise man' (*Parson's Tale*, 10.664). He is cited extensively as an authority and fount of trustworthy counsel in *The Tale of Melibee*. For Luther, Solomon is the

'Wise Man' (*Works*, 1955–57, 45.306), a type of Christ (14.327), and a magus, having 'secret knowledge of nature' (52.161).

Solomon appears principally as the great castigator of human folly and ignorance in Renaissance literature. If Tottel's *Miscellany* of 1557 takes Solomon for a 'sober wit' (Arber ed., 1870, 168), Sir Thomas Browne is less restrained: his *Religio Medici* counsels its reader to follow Solomon's advice (Proverbs 6:6) and go to insects for genuine wisdom (1.16). In Butler's *Hudibras*, a lady contrasts contemporary fools with the ancient Solomon (3.195). More directly constructive, Bacon's *New Atlantis* envisions a program of empirical sciences in the 'House of Solomon'. Bunyan works out a typology in *Solomon's Temple Spiritualized*. For the major neoclassical satirists from Dryden to Johnson, Horace or Juvenal rather than Solomon provides the exemplary analogue of the combatant against vanity, unreason, and the realm of dunces.

The Solomon of the 19th century comes in many guises. Walter Scott's *Anne of Geierstein* recalls the man of wit so unlike the fool (chapter 30); and Dickens refers to 'sentiment... Solomonic' in *Little Dorrit* (1.13) and in *Dombey and Son* has his Captain Cuttle make a warmhearted philanthropist of Solomon, quick to share a good bottle with the less fortunate (chapter 15). By contrast, the last paragraph of Thackeray's *Vanity Fair* calls up the sombre wisdom of Solomon's Ecclesiastes: 'Ah! *Vanitas Vanitatum!*' In Browning's 'Mr Sludge, "The Medium,"' the charlatan caught in a deception turns the moral indignation of his superficial Boston patron back on the accuser, pronouncing as the most hateful form of foolery that of 'the social sage, Solomon of saloons / And philosophic diner-out' (773–74). A story of 'Wisdom in the abstract facing Folly in the concrete' (chapter 13), Hardy's *Far from the Madding Crowd* alludes to Solomon as misogynist (chapter 22) and womanizer (chapter 7). 'The Preacher' is enlisted as an ally of scientific and artistic culture in the 'Conclusion' of Arnold's *Literature and Dogma*: the proposition that God 'hath set the world' in the 'heart' (Ecclesiastes 3:11) advances the argument that the Bible is symbolic rather than dogmatic in design. In *King Solomon's Mines*, a popular romance of fabulous hidden wealth and exotic adventure, H. Rider Haggard exploits another memory of that monarch.

Melville centers his entire work after *Typee* and *Omoo* on Solomon's view of earthly wisdom as folly. 'I read Solomon more &

more, and every time see deeper & deeper and unspeakable meanings in him,' he writes to Hawthorne (Leyda, *The Melville Log*, 1951, 1.413). In *Moby Dick*, the sceptical Ishmael invokes the 'unchristian Solomon's wisdom' in confirmation of the nullity he perceives at the centre of the entire creation: 'the truest of all books is Solomon's, and Ecclesiastes is the fine hammered steel of woe. "All is vanity". ALL' (chapter 96). The blank, perfectly balanced stone signed 'Solomon the Wise,' which encapsulates Melville's theme in *Pierre, or The Ambiguities*, is a text devoid of all light: the reflexive logic of the sceptic's foolish wisdom is self-cancelling. Such annihilating doubt is alien to Solomon Swap, Lot Sap Sago, and Jonathan Ploughboy, the shrewd, homely Yankee characters of the early 19th-century popular American stage who were derived from Solomon Gundy, the French Cockney of George Colman the Younger's *Who Wants a Guinea?* The stories of 'ole King Sollermun' in Twain's *Huckleberry Finn* serve to poke fun at more than just the languor and unprofitableness of royalty. The 'learned' Huck recalls that Solomon 'had about a million wives,' and the wise Jim, who understandably reckons Solomon a fool for having a 'harem' of that size, foolishly misconstrues that king's most celebrated act of judicial wisdom (chapter 14).

In Conrad's *Typhoon*, a tale of wise ignorance or ignorant wisdom, the avuncular and enlightened chief engineer, Mr Solomon Rout, 'Old Sol,' who rarely sees the light of day, writes entertaining letters filled with sagacious observations comically mistaken for his biblical namesake's. By tale's end, he finds that his obtuse captain, MacWhirr, who writes uninspired letters, is a rather wise and clever man. More recently, the Solomon of Langston Hughes' poem 'Brass Spittoons' delights in wine cups, like the reveller of James Ball Naylor's *Ancient Authors*:

> King David and King Solomon
>   Led merry, merry lives,
> With many, many lady friends
>   And many, many wives.

Camille R. La Bossière
University of Ottawa
Jerry A. Gladson
Psychological Studies Institute, Atlanta, Georgia

Tower of Ivory

In the wealth of oriental imagery which constitutes the praise of the beloved woman in the Song of Solomon is included the simile, 'Thy neck is as a tower of ivory' (Song of Solomon 7:4; cf. 4:4). For many of the early Fathers of the church (e.g., Cassiodorus, Philo of Carpasia), the tower represents the church, and the 'ivory' by which it is fortified is the whiteness and purity of its priests. The tower is also sometimes said to be 'the knowledge of Scripture' (Philo of Carpasia), or that obedience which fitly joins the mystical Body of Christ with its Head.

As part of a conventional biblical description of the beautiful woman, this phrase was frequently borrowed in medieval secular poetry. Chaucer's Black Knight describes his lost love to the Dreamer in imagery drawn from the Song of Solomon: 'Hyr throte, as I have now memoyre, / Semed a round tour of yvoyre, / Of good gretnesse, and noght to gret' (*Book of the Duchess*, 945–47). In a bizarre Renaissance adaptation, the 'fair Serena' in book 6 of Spenser's *Faerie Queene* is stripped naked by cannibals, who then 'with their eyes the daintiest morsels chose,' including prominently 'her yvorie neck; her alabaster brest' (6.8.39, 42).

In elaborate concordances of symbols for the Virgin Mary, such as that compiled by St Anthony of Padua, the tower of ivory (Vulgate *turris eburnea*) is taken to signify the strength and purity of Mary's virginity (*In Annuntiatione Sanctae Mariae*, 3), following a tradition already established by St Bernard of Clairvaux (*Corona Beatae Mariae Virginis*). This kind of allegorizing of the Song of Solomon to praise the Virgin was sharply rejected by several of the Reformers, and those parts of the Litany of the Virgin which included such references were dropped from Cranmer's *Book of Common Prayer*.

The phrase is often employed in modern literature in self-conscious reflection of late medieval tradition. In Oscar Wilde's *Salome,* the title character teases and taunts Jokanaan (John the Baptist) in his dungeon with variations of the oriental lover's vocabulary, underscoring Wilde's parodic intent: 'It is thy mouth that I desire, Jokanaan. Thy mouth is like a band of scarlet on a tower of ivory.' Swinburne's poem 'Dolores,' addressed to 'Our Lady of Pain,' is another sacral parody: 'O garden where all men may dwell, / O

tower not ivory, but builded / By hands that reach heaven from hell.'
At Christmas dinner Dante tells Joyce's Stephen (*A Portrait of the Artist as a Young Man,* chapter 1) not to play with Protestants, because they mock the litany of the Blessed Virgin: '*Tower of Ivory,* they used to say, *House of Gold!*' His comment causes Stephen to think of a Protestant girl, Eileen, with 'long, thin, cool white hands... like ivory, only soft. That was the meaning of *Tower of Ivory* but Protestants could not understand it and made fun of it... Her fair hair... gold in the sun. *Tower of Ivory, House of Gold.* By thinking of things you could understand them.'

David L. Jeffrey
University of Ottawa

Voice of the Turtle

Actually, the turtledove, or mourning dove (Song of Solomon 2:12); its call to love is parodied by Chaucer in his *Merchant's Tale,* where old Januarie beckons his young wife out into his enclosed garden with lines more familiar to medieval readers for their allegorical association with the Bridegroom and his eternal Bride:

> Rys up, my wyf, my love, my lady free!
> The turtles voyse is herd, my dowve sweete;
> The wynter is goon with alle his reynes weete.
> (4.2138–40)

David L. Jeffrey
University of Ottawa

THE SONG OF SOLOMON

The song of songs, which is Solomon's.

Beloved

> Let him kiss me with the kisses of his mouth:
>> for thy love is better than wine.
> Because of the savour of thy good ointments
>> thy name is as ointment poured forth,
>> therefore do the virgins love thee.
> Draw me, we will run after thee:
>> the king hath brought me into his chambers.

Chorus

> We will be glad and rejoice in thee,
>> we will remember thy love more than wine:
> the upright love thee.

Beloved

> I am black, but comely,
>> O ye daughters of Jerusalem,
>> as the tents of Kedar,
>> as the curtains of Solomon.
> Look not upon me, because I am black,
>> because the sun hath looked upon me:
> my mother's children were angry with me;
>> they made me the keeper of the vineyards;
>> but mine own vineyard have I not kept.
> Tell me, O thou whom my soul loveth, where thou feedest,
>> where thou makest thy flock to rest at noon:
> for why should I be as one that turneth aside
>> by the flocks of thy companions?

Chorus

If thou know not, O thou fairest among women,
　　go thy way forth by the footsteps of the flock,
and feed thy kids beside the shepherds' tents.

Lover

I have compared thee, O my love,
　　to a company of horses in Pharaoh's chariots.
Thy cheeks are comely with rows of jewels,
　　thy neck with chains of gold.
We will make thee borders of gold
　　with studs of silver.

Beloved

While the king sitteth at his table,
　　my spikenard sendeth forth the smell thereof.
A bundle of myrrh is my well-beloved unto me;
　　he shall lie all night betwixt my breasts.
My beloved is unto me as a cluster of camphire
　　in the vineyards of Engedi.

Lover

Behold, thou art fair, my love;
　　behold, thou art fair;
　　thou hast doves' eyes.

Beloved

Behold, thou art fair, my beloved,
　　yea, pleasant:
　　also our bed is green.

Lover

The beams of our house are cedar,
　　and our rafters of fir.

Beloved

> I am the rose of Sharon,
>> and the lily of the valleys.

Lover

> As the lily among thorns,
>> so is my love among the daughters.

Beloved

> As the apple tree among the trees of the wood,
>> so is my beloved among the sons.
> I sat down under his shadow with great delight,
>> and his fruit was sweet to my taste.
> He brought me to the banqueting house,
>> and his banner over me was love.
> Stay me with flagons,
>> comfort me with apples:
>> for I am sick of love.
> His left hand is under my head,
>> and his right hand doth embrace me.
> I charge you, O ye daughters of Jerusalem,
>> by the roes, and by the hinds of the field,
> that ye stir not up, nor awake my love,
>> till he please.

> The voice of my beloved!
>> behold, he cometh
> leaping upon the mountains,
>> skipping upon the hills.
> My beloved is like a roe or a young hart:
>> behold, he standeth behind our wall,
> he looketh forth at the windows,
>> shewing himself through the lattice.

> My beloved spake, and said unto me,
>> Rise up, my love,
>> my fair one, and come away.

For, lo, the winter is past,
    the rain is over and gone;
The flowers appear on the earth;
    the time of the singing of birds is come,
and the voice of the turtle
    is heard in our land;
The fig tree putteth forth her green figs,
    and the vines with the tender grape give a good smell.
Arise, my love,
    my fair one, and come away.

Lover

O my dove, that art in the clefts of the rock,
    in the secret places of the stairs,
let me see thy countenance,
    let me hear thy voice;
for sweet is thy voice,
    and thy countenance is comely.
Take us the foxes,
    the little foxes,
that spoil the vines:
    for our vines have tender grapes.

Beloved

My beloved is mine, and I am his:
    he feedeth among the lilies.
Until the day break,
    and the shadows flee away,
turn, my beloved,
    and be thou like a roe
or a young hart
    upon the mountains of Bether.

By night on my bed
I sought him whom my soul loveth:
I sought him, but I found him not.

I will rise now, and go about the city
   in the streets, and in the broad ways
I will seek him whom my soul loveth:
   I sought him, but I found him not.

The watchmen that go about the city found me:
   to whom I said, Saw ye him whom my soul loveth?
It was but a little that I passed from them,
   but I found him whom my soul loveth:
I held him, and would not let him go,
   until I had brought him into my mother's house,
   and into the chamber of her that conceived me.
I charge you, O ye daughters of Jerusalem,
   by the roes, and by the hinds of the field,
that ye stir not up, nor awake my love,
   till he please.

Who is this that cometh out of the wilderness
   like pillars of smoke,
perfumed with myrrh and frankincense,
   with all powders of the merchant?
Behold his bed, which is Solomon's;
   threescore valiant men are about it,
   of the valiant of Israel.
They all hold swords,
   being expert in war:
every man hath his sword upon his thigh
   because of fear in the night.
King Solomon made himself a chariot
   of the wood of Lebanon.
He made the pillars thereof of silver,
   the bottom thereof of gold,
the covering of it of purple,
   the midst thereof being paved with love,
for the daughters of Jerusalem.
Go forth, O ye daughters of Zion,
   and behold king Solomon with the crown
   wherewith his mother crowned him

in the day of his espousals,
    and in the day of the gladness of his heart.

Lover

Behold, thou art fair, my love;
    behold, thou art fair;
    thou hast doves' eyes within thy locks:
thy hair is as a flock of goats,
    that appear from mount Gilead.
Thy teeth are like a flock of sheep that are even shorn,
    which came up from the washing;
whereof every one bear twins,
    and none is barren among them.
Thy lips are like a thread of scarlet,
    and thy speech is comely:
thy temples are like a piece of a pomegranate
    within thy locks.
Thy neck is like the tower of David
    builded for an armoury,
whereon there hang a thousand bucklers,
    all shields of mighty men.
Thy two breasts are like two young roes
    that are twins,
    which feed among the lilies.
Until the day break,
    and the shadows flee away,
I will get me to the mountain of myrrh,
    and to the hill of frankincense.
Thou art all fair, my love;
    there is no spot in thee.

Come with me from Lebanon, my spouse,
    with me from Lebanon:
look from the top of Amana,
    from the top of Shenir and Hermon,
from the lions' dens,
    from the mountains of the leopards.

Thou hast ravished my heart, my sister, my spouse;
   thou hast ravished my heart
with one of thine eyes,
   with one chain of thy neck.
How fair is thy love, my sister, my spouse!
   how much better is thy love than wine!
   and the smell of thine ointments than all spices!
Thy lips, O my spouse, drop as the honeycomb:
   honey and milk are under thy tongue;
   and the smell of thy garments is like the smell of Lebanon.
A garden inclosed is my sister, my spouse;
   a spring shut up, a fountain sealed.
Thy plants are an orchard of pomegranates,
   with pleasant fruits;
   camphire, with spikenard,
   Spikenard and saffron;
   calamus and cinnamon,
   with all trees of frankincense;
   myrrh and aloes,
   with all the chief spices:
A fountain of gardens,
   a well of living waters,
   and streams from Lebanon.

Beloved

Awake, O north wind;
   and come, thou south;
blow upon my garden,
   that the spices thereof may flow out.
Let my beloved come into his garden,
   and eat his pleasant fruits.

Lover

I am come into my garden, my sister, my spouse:
I have gathered my myrrh with my spice;
I have eaten my honeycomb with my honey;
   I have drunk my wine with my milk.

Chorus

Eat, O friends; drink,
  yea, drink abundantly, O beloved.

Beloved

I sleep, but my heart waketh:
  it is the voice of my beloved that knocketh, saying,
Open to me, my sister, my love,
  my dove, my undefiled:
for my head is fillèd with dew,
  and my locks with the drops of the night.
I have put off my coat;
  how shall I put it on?
I have washed my feet;
  how shall I defile them?
My beloved put in his hand by the hole of the door,
  and my bowels were moved for him.
I rose up to open to my beloved;
  and my hands dropped with myrrh,
and my fingers with sweet smelling myrrh,
  upon the handles of the lock.
I opened to my beloved;
  but my beloved had withdrawn himself, and was gone:
  my soul failed when he spake:
I sought him, but I could not find him;
  I called him, but he gave me no answer.
The watchmen that went about the city found me,
  they smote me, they wounded me;
  the keepers of the walls took away my veil from me.
I charge you, O daughters of Jerusalem,
  if ye find my beloved,
that ye tell him,
  that I am sick of love.

Chorus

What is thy beloved more than another beloved,
  O thou fairest among women?

what is thy beloved more than another beloved,
    that thou dost so charge us?

Beloved

My beloved is white and ruddy,
    the chiefest among ten thousand.
His head is as the most fine gold,
    his locks are bushy,
    and black as a raven.
His eyes are as the eyes of doves
    by the rivers of waters,
washed with milk,
    and fitly set.
His cheeks are as a bed of spices,
    as sweet flowers:
his lips like lilies,
    dropping sweet smelling myrrh.
His hands are as gold rings
    set with the beryl:
his belly is as bright ivory
    overlaid with sapphires.
His legs are as pillars of marble,
    set upon sockets of fine gold:
his countenance is as Lebanon,
    excellent as the cedars.
His mouth is most sweet:
    yea, he is altogether lovely.
This is my beloved, and this is my friend,
    O daughters of Jerusalem.

Chorus

Whither is thy beloved gone,
O thou fairest among women?
whither is thy beloved turned aside?
    that we may seek him with thee.

Beloved

My beloved is gone down into his garden,
    to the beds of spices,
to feed in the gardens,
    and to gather lilies.
I am my beloved's, and my beloved is mine:
    he feedeth among the lilies.

Lover

Thou art beautiful, O my love, as Tirzah,
    comely as Jerusalem,
    terrible as an army with banners.
Turn away thine eyes from me,
    for they have overcome me:
thy hair is as a flock of goats
    that appear from Gilead.
Thy teeth are as a flock of sheep
    which go up from the washing,
whereof every one beareth twins,
    and there is not one barren among them.
As a piece of a pomegranate
    are thy temples within thy locks.
There are threescore queens,
    and fourscore concubines,
    and virgins without number.
My dove, my undefiled is but one;
    she is the only one of her mother,
    she is the choice one of her that bare her.
The daughters saw her, and blessed her;
    yea, the queens and the concubines,
    and they praised her.

Chorus

Who is she that looketh forth as the morning,
    fair as the moon, clear as the sun,
    and terrible as an army with banners?

Lover

I went down into the garden of nuts
    to see the fruits of the valley,
and to see whether the vine flourished
    and the pomegranates budded.
Or ever I was aware,
    my soul made me like the chariots of Amminadib.

Chorus

Return, return, O Shulamite;
    return, return, that we may look upon thee.

Lover

What will ye see in the Shulamite?
    As it were the company of two armies.
How beautiful are thy feet with shoes,
    O prince's daughter!
the joints of thy thighs are like jewels,
    the work of the hands of a cunning workman.
Thy navel is like a round goblet,
    which wanteth not liquor:
thy belly is like an heap of wheat
    set about with lilies.
Thy two breasts are like two young roes
    that are twins.
Thy neck is as a tower of ivory;
thine eyes like the fishpools in Heshbon,
    by the gate of Bathrabbim:
thy nose is as the tower of Lebanon
    which looketh toward Damascus.
Thine head upon thee is like Carmel,
    and the hair of thine head like purple;
    the king is held in the galleries.
How fair and how pleasant art thou,
    O love, for delights!

This thy stature is like to a palm tree,
    and thy breasts to clusters of grapes.
I said, I will go up to the palm tree,
    I will take hold of the boughs thereof:
now also thy breasts shall be as clusters of the vine,
    and the smell of thy nose like apples;
    And the roof of thy mouth like the best wine.

Beloved

For my beloved, that goeth down sweetly,
    causing the lips of those that are asleep to speak.
I am my beloved's,
    and his desire is toward me.
Come, my beloved, let us go forth into the field;
    let us lodge in the villages.
Let us get up early to the vineyards;
    let us see if the vine flourish,
whether the tender grape appear,
    and the pomegranates bud forth:
    there will I give thee my loves.
The mandrakes give a smell,
    and at our gates are all manner of pleasant fruits,
new and old,
    which I have laid up for thee, O my beloved.

O that thou wert as my brother,
    that sucked the breasts of my mother!
when I should find thee without,
    I would kiss thee;
    yea, I should not be despised.
I would lead thee,
    and bring thee into my mother's house,
    who would instruct me:
I would cause thee to drink of spiced wine
    of the juice of my pomegranate.
His left hand should be under my head,
    and his right hand should embrace me.

I charge you, O daughters of Jerusalem,
    that ye stir not up, nor awake my love,
    until he please.

Chorus

Who is this that cometh up from the wilderness,
    leaning upon her beloved?

Beloved

I raised thee up under the apple tree:
    there thy mother brought thee forth:
    there she brought thee forth that bare thee.
Set me as a seal upon thine heart,
    as a seal upon thine arm:
for love is strong as death;
    jealousy is cruel as the grave:
the coals thereof are coals of fire,
    which hath a most vehement flame.
Many waters cannot quench love,
    neither can the floods drown it:
if a man would give
    all the substance of his house for love,
    it would utterly be contemned.

Chorus

We have a little sister,
    and she hath no breasts:
what shall we do for our sister
    in the day when she shall be spoken for?
If she be a wall,
    we will build upon her a palace of silver:
and if she be a door,
    we will inclose her with boards of cedar.

Beloved

I am a wall,
    and my breasts like towers:
then was I in his eyes
    as one that found favour.
Solomon had a vineyard at Baalhamon;
    he let out the vineyard unto keepers;
every one for the fruit thereof
    was to bring a thousand pieces of silver.
My vineyard, which is mine, is before me:
    thou, O Solomon, must have a thousand,
    and those that keep the fruit thereof two hundred.

Lover

Thou that dwellest in the gardens,
    the companions hearken to thy voice:
    cause me to hear it.

Beloved

Make haste, my beloved,
    and be thou like to a roe
or to a young hart
    upon the mountains of spices.

Index of Primary Sources